Leopard's Guide to Keeping Clean

Published in 2026 by Windmill Books,
an Imprint of Rosen Publishing
2544 Clinton St.
Buffalo, NY 14224

First published in Great Britain in 2022 by Hodder & Stoughton

Credits
Commissioning editor: Sarah Peutrill
Series editor: Lisa Edwards
Series Designer: Rachel Lawston

Cataloging-in-Publication Data
Names: Edwards, Lisa, author. | Roberts, Sian, illustrator.
Title: Leopard's guide to keeping clean / Lisa Edwards, illustrated by Sian Roberts.
Description: Buffalo, NY : Windmill Books, 2026. | Series: Healthy habits
Identifiers: ISBN 9781538399644 (pbk.) | ISBN 9781538399651 (library bound) | ISBN 9781538399668 (ebook)
Subjects: LCSH: Hygiene--Juvenile literature. | Health attitudes--Juvenile literature. | Leopard--Juvenile literature.
Classification: LCC RA780.E393 2026 | DDC 613.4--dc23

Printed in the United States of America

CPSIA Compliance Information: Batch #CSWM26
For Further Information contact Rosen Publishing at 1-800-237-9932

Healthy Habits

Leopard's Guide to Keeping Clean

Lisa Edwards

Siân Roberts

WINDMILL BOOKS

Leopard and her cubs are meeting
the other animals at the waterhole.

It's time for all the animals to drink and wash up. They know how important it is to keep clean.

There are tiny living things all around us. We can't see them, but they can make us very sick if they get inside our bodies. They are called germs.

You need to make sure your body is clean and free from germs.

Leopard spends around half her day making sure her cubs are nice and clean.

Leopard uses her bristly tongue and teeth to clean her cubs' fur thoroughly. It helps to remove germs, bad smells, and insects.

You can easily spread germs on your hands. You need to wash your hands with soap and water regularly, making sure you clean in between fingers and the backs of your hands.

Leopard and her family have bodies that are designed to fight off germs, especially from the meat they eat.

You need to wash your hands with soap and water before you eat food.

This helps to stop germs from getting into your food and then into your body. It's also a good idea to wash your hands after playing outside - especially if you get as muddy as Elephant!

Clean your teeth regularly to keep your teeth and gums healthy and free from germs. It's best to brush your teeth for two minutes in the morning and at night.

Leopard doesn't have a toothbrush! Her teeth are cleaned when she chews meat. The bones in the meat help to keep her and the cubs' teeth clean.

It's important to cover your nose and mouth with a tissue or a face-covering when you sneeze or cough. This makes sure you are not spreading any germs to others.

It would be hard to find a tissue big enough for Elephant!

When they play, Leopard's cubs like to chase and pounce on each other.

Leopard will have to clean them up when they've finished.

If you've been exercising, it's very important to wash away any dirt afterward. Germs love dirt!

When you bathe or shower you remove dirt, oil, sweat, and germs that can make you smell.

Bathing your whole body with warm water and soap will make you smell good again.

Leopard grooms her cubs every single day so that they are fresh and clean. When they are older, they will swim with her.

Leopard makes sure she cleans every part of each of her cubs. She turns it into playtime to make it more fun!

Some areas of your body need extra cleaning because it's easier for germs to get trapped there.

Make sure you clean properly under your arms, between your legs and toes, and behind your ears.

When she licks her cubs, leopard removes any loose fur. It's a good idea to wash your hair at least once or twice a week to remove dirt and oils where germs can live.

Leopard's cubs now have the same golden fur and dark spots as their mom. When they were born, they had grey fur and blue eyes! Have your eyes or hair changed since you were a baby?

It's important to keep fingernails and toenails clean and trimmed to stop germs from living in and under them.

Bath time is usually best for doing this - ask an adult to help you.

Leopard uses her claws only when she needs them - to hunt another animal or to climb a tree. Just like a pet cat, she pulls her claws back into her paws when she isn't using them.

Leopard cleans the cubs' fur every day to remove smells that can attract predators.

Wearing clean socks, underwear, and clothes can help you stay clean after you've had a bath or a shower. Make sure you are completely dry before you put them on!

Leopard has been showing us how she keeps herself and her cubs clean. How can you keep clean?

Wash your hands regularly

Wash your hands before you eat

Keep your mouth and teeth clean

Cover your nose and mouth when you cough and sneeze

Wash after exercise

Take a regular bath or shower

Wash your whole body

Wash your hair regularly

Keep your nails clean

Wear clean clothes

Glossary

Bristly covered with short, stiff hairs. A leopard's tongue bristles are made from the same material as your fingernails!

Germs a tiny living thing which cannot be seen by a human eye but can cause disease.

Groom to brush or clean the fur of an animal.

Predators animals that hunt and kill other animals for food.

Waterhole a place where water collects, especially in a dry country, where animals gather to drink.

Let's talk about healthy habits...

The *Healthy Habits* series has been been written to help young children begin to understand how they can live healthy lives, both in their relationships with others and in their own bodies.

It provides a starting point for parents, caregivers, and teachers to discuss healthy ways of being in the world with little learners. The series involves a cast of animal characters who behave in healthy ways in their own habitats, relating their experiences to familiar, everyday scenarios for children.

Leopard's Guide to Keeping Clean

This story looks at all the ways you can make sure you are keeping yourself clean and healthy.

The book aims to encourage a child's awareness of the importance of washing regularly and keeping germs at bay to prevent disease. It offers children a simple checklist of cleaning activities that can keep their whole body free from germs.

How to use the book:

The book is designed for adults to share with either an individual child, or a group of children, and as a starting point for discussion.

Choose a time when both you and the children are relaxed and have time to share the story.

Before reading the story:

- Spend time looking at the illustrations and talking about what the book might be about before reading it together. Ask the children to look at the details in each picture to see what all the creatures are doing – some of them are echoing the main themes in the background of the story.
- Encourage children to employ a "phonics-first" approach to tackling new words by sounding them out.

After reading the story:

- Talk about the story with the children. Ask them to list occasions when they are asked to wash their hands, such as before a meal. Why do they think it's important to do so?
- Discuss the existence of germs with the children. Do they cover their faces when they cough or sneeze? Why do they think it's important? You can discuss the idea of protecting others from your germs.
- Place the children into four groups – one for washing hands (and nails), cleaning teeth, taking a bath or shower, and washing hair. Ask them to write a clear list of instructions for the other groups on the best way to execute each cleanliness step.
- At the end of the session, discuss each cleanliness step with the whole class. Finish by talking about the importance of wearing clean clothes after bathing – to keep germs at bay for longer.

Healthy Habits

TITLES IN THIS SERIES

DOG'S GUIDE TO HELPING OTHERS

ELEPHANT'S GUIDE TO MAKING FRIENDS

KANGAROO'S GUIDE TO KEEPING FIT

KOALA'S GUIDE TO SLEEP

LEMUR'S GUIDE TO HEALTHY EATING

LEOPARD'S GUIDE TO KEEPING CLEAN

PANDA'S GUIDE TO MENTAL WELL-BEING

SLOTH'S GUIDE TO KEEPING CALM

WINDMILL BOOKS™

ISBN: 9781538399644

9 781538 399644